On a Wing AND a Prayer

paintings by the
HAUTMAN BROTHERS

HARVEST HOUSE PUBLISHERS

EUGENE, OREGON

On a Wing and a Prayer

Text copyright © 2006 by Harvest House Publishers
Published by Harvest House Publishers
Eugene, Oregon 97402

ISBN-13: 978-0-7369-1794-0
ISBN-10: 0-7369-1794-2

Artwork designs are reproduced under license from © 2006 by The Hautman
Brothers, courtesy of MHS Licensing, and may not be reproduced without permission.

Design and production by Koechel Peterson & Associates, Inc., Minneapolis, MN

Harvest House Publishers has made every effort to trace the ownership of all poems
and quotes. In the event of a question arising from the use of a poem or quote, we
regret any error made and will be pleased to make the necessary correction in future
editions of this book.

Verses are taken from the HOLY BIBLE, NEW INTERNATIONAL VERSION®,
NIV®. Copyright © 1973, 1978, 1984 by the International Bible Society. Used by
permission of Zondervan. All rights reserved.

Printed in China

08 09 10 11 12 13 / LP / 10 9 8 7 6 5 4

He tends his flock like a shepherd:

He gathers the lambs

in his arms and carries

them close to his heart.

The Book of Isaiah

God writes with a pen that never blots,
speaks with a tongue that never slips,
and acts with a hand that never fails.

Author Unknown

May true friends be around you.
Of all that is near,
Thou are the nearest.
Of all that is dear,
Thou are the dearest.

AUTHOR UNKNOWN

Hope Is a Thing with Feathers

Hope is a thing with feathers
That perches in the soul
And sings a tune without words
And never stops at all.

And sweetest, in the gale, is heard
And sore must be the storm
That could abash the little bird
That keeps so many warm.

I've heard it in the chilliest land
And on the strangest sea
Yet, never, in extremity
It ask a crumb of me.

EMILY DICKINSON

You will never understand why God does what He does, but if you believe Him, that is all that is necessary. Let us learn to trust for who He is.

ELISABETH ELLIOT

THE SHEPHERD KNOWS what pastures are best for his sheep, and they must not question nor doubt, but trustingly follow Him. Perhaps He sees that the best pastures for some of us are to be found in the midst of opposition or of earthly trials. If He leads you there, you may be sure they are green for you, and you will grow and be made strong by feeding there. Perhaps He sees that the best waters for you to walk beside will be raging waves of trouble and sorrow. If this should be the case, He will make them still waters for you, and you must go and lie down beside them, and let them have all their blessed influences upon you.

HANNAH WHITALL SMITH

God beholds thee individually, whoever thou art. "He calls thee by thy name." He sees thee, and understands thee. He knows what is in thee, all thy own peculiar feelings and thoughts, thy dispositions and likings, thy strength and thy weakness. He views thee in thy day of rejoicing and thy day of sorrow. He sympathizes in thy hopes and in thy temptations; He interests himself in all thy anxieties and thy remembrances, in all the risings and fallings of thy spirit. He compasses thee round, and bears thee in His arms; He takes thee up and sets thee down. Thou dost not love thyself better than He loves thee.

JOHN H. NEWMAN

Know that the LORD is God.

It is he who made us,

and we are his;

we are his people,

the sheep of his pasture.

The Book of Psalms

Grant us Thy peace, down from Thy presence falling,
As on the thirsty earth cool night-dews sweet;
Grant us Thy peace, to Thy pure paths recalling,
From devious ways, our worn and wandering feet.

ELIZA SCUDDER

He who cares for the lily,

And heeds the sparrows' fall,

Shall tenderly lead His loving child:

For He made and loveth all.

Author Unknown

Sometimes, at night, it was almost as if I could hear the assurance that God the Father gave to another soldier, named Joshua: "I will not fail thee nor forsake thee."

GEN. MATTHEW B. RIDGEWAY

Are we weak and heavy laden,
cumbered with a load of care?
Precious Savior, still our refuge,
take it to the Lord in prayer.
Do your friends despise, forsake you?
Take it to the Lord in prayer!
In His arms He'll take and shield you;
you will find a solace there.

JOSEPH SCRIVEN

GOD'S MARK OF APPROVAL, whenever you obey Him,
is peace. He sends an immeasurable, deep peace; not a
natural peace, "as the world gives," but the peace of Jesus.
Whenever peace does not come, wait until it does.

OSWALD CHAMBERS

To grow tall in your faith, root your life in prayer.

Author Unknown

There is a comfort in the strength of love;
'Twill make a thing endurable, which else
Would overset the brain, or break the heart…

William Wordsworth

❦

He leadeth me, O blessed thought,
O words with heavenly comfort fraught,
Whate'er I do, where'er I be,
Still 'tis God's hand that leadeth me.

JOSEPH HENRY GILMORE

God does not lead His children
around hardship, but leads them
straight through hardship. But He
leads! And amidst the hardship,
He is nearer to them than ever before.

OTTO DIBELIUS

Do not be anxious about

anything, but in everything,

by prayer and petition,

with thanksgiving, present your

requests to God. And the peace

of God, which transcends

all understanding, will guard

your hearts and your minds

in Jesus Christ.

The Book of Philippians

Any concern too small
to be turned into a prayer is too small
to be made into a burden.

CORRIE TEN BOOM

Let nothing disturb thee,

Let nothing affright thee,

All things are passing,

God changeth never.

Henry Wadsworth Longfellow

⁓ ∘ ⁓

Happiness is peace after strife,

the overcoming of difficulties,

the feeling of security and well-being.

H.L. Mencken

For answered prayer we thank You, Lord,

We know You're always there

To hear us when we call on You;

We're grateful for Your care.

J. David Branon

> *God answers sharp and*
> *sudden on some prayers,*
> *and thrusts the thing we have*
> *prayed for in our face,*
> *a gauntlet with a gift in it.*

Elizabeth Barrett Browning

Prayer increases our ability to accept the present moment. You cannot live in the future, you cannot live in the past, you can only live in the now. The present moment is already exactly as it ought to be, even if we do not understand why it is as it is.

Matthew Kelly

My secret is simple. I pray.

Mother Teresa

When the trials of this life make you weary
And your troubles seem too much to bear,
There's a wonderful solace and comfort
In the silent communion of prayer.

AUTHOR UNKNOWN

When comforts are declining,
    He grants the soul again
    A season of clear shining,
    To cheer it after rain.

WILLIAM COWPER

He leads me where the waters glide,
The waters soft and still,
And homeward He will gently guide
My wandering heart and will.

JOHN KEBLE

God has not promised skies always blue,

Flower-strewn pathways all our lives through;

God has not promised sun without rain,

Joy without sorrow, peace without pain.

But God has promised strength for the day,

Rest for the labor, light for the way,

Grace for the trials, help from above,

Unfailing sympathy, undying love.

Annie Johnson Flint

O God, make us children
of quietness and heirs of peace.

CLEMENT OF ROME

How priceless is your unfailing love!
Both high and low among men
find refuge in the shadow of your wings.

THE BOOK OF PSALMS

*A*n infinite God can give all of Himself

to each of His children. He does not

distribute Himself that each may have a

part, but to each one He gives all of

Himself as fully as if there were no others.

A.W. Tozer

Take the Name of Jesus with you,
Child of sorrow and of woe,
It will joy and comfort give you;
Take it then, where'er you go.

LYDIA BAXTER

I do not ask to walk

smooth paths nor bear an easy load.

I pray for strength and fortitude

to climb the rock strewn road.

Give me such courage and I can scale

the hardest peaks alone,

And transform every stumbling

block into a stepping stone.

Gale Brook Burket

❖

God comforts us on every side.
THE BOOK OF PSALMS

God is in control of all outcomes
as well as in control of the process.

Merilyn Thompson

God, who gives us His peace, extends rest to the weary and renewal to the exhausted. He wants our souls to be at peace, and He promises to accomplish that peace.

ELIZABETH GEORGE

Just When My Hopes Are Vanished

Just when my hopes are vanished,

Just when my friends forsake,

Just when the fight is thickest,

Just when with fear I shake—

Then comes a still small whisper:

"Fear not, My child, I'm near."

Jesus brings peace and comfort,

I love His voice to hear.

J. Bruce Evans

Under His wings, what a refuge in sorrow!

How the heart yearningly turns to His rest!

Often when earth has no balm for my healing,

There I find comfort, and there I am blessed.

William Cushing

May your unfailing love be my comfort, according to your promise to your servant. Let your compassion come to me that I may live, for your law is my delight.

The Book of Psalms

Comfort can be found in a variety of things—food, family,
memories, friends—but I continue to receive the most comfort from
our heavenly Father as I journey through the Scriptures.

EMILIE BARNES

Prayer means that the total you is praying.
Your whole being reaches out to God,
and God reaches down to you...

E. Stanley Jones

❧

SHE COULD NOT SPEAK, but she did "hold on," and

the warm grasp of the friendly human hand comforted

her sore heart, and seemed to lead her nearer to the Divine

arm which alone could uphold her in her trouble.

LOUISA MAY ALCOTT

Do what you can do, and
pray for what you cannot do.

Saint Augustine

Lord help me live from day to day

In such a self-forgetful way,

That even when I kneel to pray,

My prayer shall be for—others.

CHARLES D. MEIGS

GOD OF LIFE, THERE ARE DAYS when the burdens we carry chafe our shoulders and wear us down; when the road seems dreary and endless, the skies gray and threatening; when our lives have no music in them and our hearts are lonely, and our souls have lost their courage. Flood the path with light, we beseech you; turn our eyes to where the skies are full of promise.

SAINT AUGUSTINE

There is a safe and sacred place
Beneath the wings divine,
Reserved for all the heirs of grace—
Oh, be that refuge mine!

Henry F. Lyte

*Ninety-eight percent of
what I worried about
never happened.*

MARK TWAIN

Grant, O God, that amidst all the
discouragements, difficulties and dangers,
distress and darkness of this mortal life,
I may depend upon thy mercy, and on this
build my hopes, as on a sure foundation.
Let thine infinite mercy in Christ Jesus
deliver me from despair…

THOMAS WILSON

*Whatever enlarges hope will
also exalt courage.*

Samuel Johnson

For joy of glowing color, flash of wings,
We thank Thee, Lord, for all the little things
That make the love and laughter of our days,
For home and happiness and friends, we praise
And thank Thee now.

Elizabeth Gould

Let this one great, gracious, glorious fact lie in your spirit until it permeates all your thoughts and makes you rejoice even though you are without strength. Rejoice that the Lord Jesus has become your strength and your song—He has become your salvation.

CHARLES SPURGEON

There is surely a
future hope for you,
and your hope will not
be cut off.

THE BOOK OF PROVERBS

God moves in a mysterious way
His wonders to perform;
He plants His footsteps in the sea
And rides upon the storm.

William Cowper

Put together all the tenderest love you
know of, the deepest you have ever
felt, and the strongest that has ever
been poured out upon you, and heap
upon it all the love of all the loving
human hearts in the world, and then
multiply it by infinity, and you will
begin, perhaps, to have some faint
glimpse of what the love of God is.

HANNAH WHITALL SMITH

What lies behind us and what lies before us are small matters compared to what lies within us.

RALPH WALDO EMERSON

We are made strong by
what we overcome.

John Burroughs

WHEN THE GREAT OAK IS straining in the wind, the boughs drink in new beauty, and the trunk sends down a deeper root on the windward side. Only the soul that knows the mighty grief can know the mighty rapture. Sorrows come to stretch out spaces in the heart for joy.

Edwin Markham

❦

All the strength and force of man
comes from his faith in things unseen.
He who believes is strong;
he who doubts is weak. Strong
convictions precede great actions.

JAMES FREEMAN CLARKE

DO NOT LOOK FORWARD TO THE changes and chances of this life in fear; rather look to them with full hope that, as they arise, God, whose you are, will deliver you out of them. He has kept you hitherto—do you but hold fast to his dear hand, and he will lead you safely through all things; and, when you cannot stand, he will bear you in his arms. Do not look forward to what may happen tomorrow; the same everlasting Father who cares for you today will take care of you tomorrow, and every day. Either he will shield you from suffering, or he will give you unfailing strength to bear it. Be at peace, then, and put aside all anxious thoughts and imaginations.

FRANCIS DE SALES

I believe in prayer.
It's the best way we have
to draw strength from heaven.

JOSEPHINE BAKER

The strength of a man consists in finding out the
way God is going, and going that way.

Henry Ward Beecher

Drop thy still dews of quietness,
  Till all our strivings cease;
Take from our souls the strain and stress,
And let our ordered lives confess
  The beauty of thy peace.

Breathe through the heats of our desire
  Thy coolness and thy balm;
Let sense be dumb, let flesh retire;
Speak through the earthquake, wind, and fire,
  O still small voice of calm.

John Greenleaf Whittier

Though the morning seems to linger
O'er the hill-tops far away,
Yet the shadows bear the promise
Of a brighter coming day.

Frances Ellen Watkins Harper

As I cross on life's tumultuous seas,
Sailing from earth to Heaven's bright shore,
Christ is like a mighty lighthouse,
Helping me to navigate my course.

He guides me safely through tides of temptation,
Over dangerous reefs of sin,
Lighting my way through dark troubled waters,
'Til the glorious port of Heaven I win.

AUTHOR UNKNOWN

*Encouragement
is oxygen to the soul.*

George M. Adams

The Shepherd Boy's Song

He that is down, needs fear no fall;
He that is low, no pride;
He that is humble ever shall
Have God to be his guide.

I am content with what I have,
Little be it or much;
And, Lord, contentment still I crave,
Because thou savest such.

Fullness to such a burden is,
That go on pilgrimage;
Here little, and hereafter bliss,
Is best from age to age.

JOHN BUNYAN

*Now faith is being sure of what we hope for
and certain of what we do not see.*

The Book of Hebrews

It is possible to begin again. It is hard
and we never do it perfectly, but it can be
done…I must begin again on joy
and happiness, on forgiveness and peace,
on gratitude and patience.

ANDREW GREELEY

Birds sing after a storm;
why shouldn't people feel as free to delight
in whatever remains to them?

Rose Kennedy